GOSPORT
IN OLD PHOTOGRAPHS

ERECTED IN 1812, THE SQUARE, COLONNADED MARKET HOUSE dominated the approach from Gosport Hard into the High Street; originally used as a market, bonding and court house, at the time this photograph was taken in 1931 it served as the offices of the Hants and Dorset bus company. The Market House was destroyed in the blitz of 1940 while the equally historic Old Northumberland Arms (left) was demolished in the 1960s during redevelopment.

GOSPORT
IN OLD PHOTOGRAPHS

COLLECTED BY
JOHN SADDEN

ALAN SUTTON

Alan Sutton Publishing Limited
Phoenix Mill · Far Thrupp · Stroud · Gloucestershire

First published 1990

British Library Cataloguing in Publication Data

Gosport in old photographs
1. Hampshire. Gosport, history
I. Sadden, John *1958–*
942.278

ISBN 0-86299-710-0

Typeset in 9/10 Korinna
Typesetting and origination by
Alan Sutton Publishing Limited.
Printed in Great Britain by
The Guernsey Press Co. Ltd.,
Guernsey, Channel Islands.

CONTENTS

INTRODUCTION

Every picture, so they say, tells a story. This charming Victorian photograph – one of the earliest depicting Gosport High Street – highlights something of the enduring strengths and ultimate limitations of that irresistible medium which has done so much to popularize local history. Taken in January 1881, possibly from the window of the India Arms Hotel, this evocative scene would not be out of place on a Christmas greetings card, reminding us of a long-lost, cosy world of gas-lamps, hot chestnuts, strong punch, log fires and traditional values. But as with the portrait on p. 65 of Edwardian children blackberrying in Rowner Copse, it is the taste of the fruit that is remembered, not the sore hands, scratched and punctured by bramble thorns; reality was different. The snowstorm of 1881 brought five-foot deep snowdrifts, the suspension of all transport and what the Portsmouth *Evening News* described as 'considerable distress'. The local coroner dealt with an increase in cases of what we now describe euphemistically as hypothermia. The poverty-stricken, the young, the old and the sick shivering in their slum dwellings a few hundred yards from where our photographer exposed his plate are left, perhaps mercifully, to the imagination.

But this is not to take anything away from the power, the immediacy and the accessibility of the photographic image. Each one is unique. In the world of the photograph lost buildings remain standing; the minutiae of everyday life are fixed in context in time; fondly remembered shops remain 'open all hours'; the departed forever gaze quizzically through the lens at us.

Gosport has been fortunate in its working photographers of the past, most notably J.C. Lawrence, H.J. Bond and W.C. Harvey, who have left us a rich diversity of material within the parameters of their commercial brief. Subjects were selected according to their sales potential and therefore crowd scenes, main streets, business establishments and group portraits figure prominently in their work. Our present, reflected view of the past, then, may be said to owe more to the market than to cultural, historical or aesthetic considerations. Nevertheless, their pictorial legacy provides the inquisitive young, the nostalgic not-so-young and the social historian with a rich and valued source of interest and pleasure.

The selection here is diverse and necessarily eclectic, having been drawn not only from the photographic archives of Gosport Museum and Gosport Library but also from the albums and attics of generous residents of the Borough, prompted into a flurry of dusty activity by the knowledge that royalties from the sale of this book are going to Gosport Community Association. One important factor in the selection was, inevitably, a desire to represent that which has been lost, and in this respect the compiler was spoilt for choice. Gosport, as we know, has lost much of its history through a combination of benign neglect (the local authority) and malign intervention (the *Luftwaffe*). Section Fifteen is comprised of examples of the latter, while on page 91 the reader will find a photograph of Gosport Railway Station.

A picture, so they say, is worth a thousand words. It is hoped that the photographs included here will act as a prompt – a starting point – rather than be an end in themselves. For if we do not share our experiences and memories, then history dies.

John Sadden
October 1990

GOSPORT GATEWAY. Haslar Arch at the end of Haslar Street was one of two constructions providing access throught he ramparts or 'Gosport Lines'. Commissioned in 1748, 'eight pieces of iron ordnance of no lesser nature than 18 pounders' were installed to defend the approaches. The other gate, at Forton, moved one contemporary writer to describe it as 'so devoid of all architectural beauty or ornament that on approaching it the mind is moved to melancholy and filled with much gloom as if entering a sepulchure or dungeon.'

SECTION ONE

On the Waterfront

VIEW OF THE ESPLANADE GARDENS in the 1930s when the fare to Portsmouth was a ha'penny at peak times and 1d. during the day.

A BUSY SCENE at the ferry booking office, about 1930.

THE ESPLANADE GARDENS were constructed in the 1920s by infilling the old Hard area, a monumental task carried out by local labour under the Government's unemployment works programme.

THE FERRY AREA was a popular haunt of opportunist pavement photographers whose uninvited attempts at naturalistic portraiture invariably met with a hostile glare or an air of self-consciously assumed indifference. Quickening their pace here (in 1931) are Agnes Cole (left) and Lilly Challen.

THE FAMILIAR CENTREPIECE and radial paths, about 1925. Admiral Gambier's old drinking fountain was removed from outside the Market House (see p. 90) and repositioned in a prominent place (left). Note the diversity of buildings fronting Beach Street, including the Alexandria Dining Rooms (see p. 153).

A UNIQUE VIEW of Gosport pontoon in 1927. A vessel is seen here attempting to recover the new forty-ton pontoon after it sank during stormy weather. The top of an electric lamp-post can be seen breaking the surface of the water. Normal service was apparently not resumed until 1930.

AN EARLY VIEW OF THE OLD COBBLED HARD, about 1910, showing the Victory Restaurant, the Isle of Wight Hoy public house and the Market House.

FLOATING BRIDGE – a fine photograph dating from the end of the last century. An observer described her affectionately as a 'chain-bound marine spirit . . . ; in other words she has no hope of freedom nor pride of appearance. She waddles across the harbour gently clucking to herself.'

A RARE AERIAL VIEW of the landing stage, showing the floating bridge (top left) in about 1950.

CAMPER & NICHOLSON'S boatbuilding sheds are visible in this earlier view from the 1930s.

A Walk up the High Street

THE HIGH STREET, viewed from the Esplanade Gardens (dated 1931), featuring the Isle of Wight Hoy public house (left). Shop awnings lined the High Street, protecting goods and customers from the weather and creating a more intimate atmosphere in which they could part with their money.

NO TRAFFIC save a rattling tram in this earlier view. Note the unself-consciously aproned woman and unhurried children.

STOPPING FOR A CHAT outside the Gosport branch of F.W. Woolworth's, the '3d. and 6d. Stores', which opened in the High Street in 1934. Next door is Clarence Cory's motor engineering workshop and, on the extreme right, the distinctive bay window of the India Arms.

A TRAM PASSES the Home and Colonial Stores (on the northern side), before passing (left to right) Gunton Bros (florists), W.B. Smith (chemist), Charles Mumby & Co. (mineral water), Mrs Holmes (newsagent), Mr Standhaft (hairdresser), Mr Tomlins (bootmaker), the Singer Sewing Machine Shop and Leonard Freake (furniture dealer). This view is dated 1929.

NORTH CROSS STREET, viewed from the High Street, in about 1925. On the left is the Bell Hotel, demolished in 1972.

LOOKING BACK down the High Street just after the turn of the century; boys in knickerbockers and girls in cotton pinafores play in the road while traders' carts are loaded up for deliveries.

IN THE SLUMP following the First World War, Lloyds Bank Ltd was granted planning permission to build a branch on the corner of North Cross Street (see facing page) with the proviso that men be taken on from Gosport Labour Exchange to carry out the work. The solid High Street façade, designed to convey reliability and substance, is seen here during the world depression of the 1930s.

PAVEMENT SCENE, about 1904. The old gentlemen are standing outside what is believed to be Hoopers, the fishmongers; the lady with the perambulator is peering into the window of Mrs Ogg's, Ladies' Outfitters, and the formidable hats and umbrellas are passing Paine and Marsh. Established in 1880, this was one of only two estate agents in the town at that time.

A HAPPY YOUNGSTER tries out his new hand-held windmill, bought from a street vendor outside the premises of Paine and Marsh (about 1930). Note the canopy of the Gosport Theatre on the left.

LOOKING BACK DOWN the High Street from Walpole Road with the Town Hall on the right, in the days when it was socially unacceptable to venture outdoors without a hat. These gentlemen are passing the old ramparts (right) which were removed in the early 1920s.

SECTION THREE

Open all Hours

ROSER'S GROCERY SHOP (formerly Kent's) in Village Road, Alverstoke, about 1927.

COLLINS' DOMESTIC BAZAAR in Forton Road, about 1920. Household equipment and kitchen utensils ranged in price from 1d. up to a maximum of 6d. (2½p). At the door is Dorothy Collins, daughter of the proprietor.

NORTH STREET ON THE EVE OF THE FIRST WORLD WAR. The sender of this postcard, 'Ada', writes to tell of her success in getting a position at Mrs Gluning's newagents and tobacconists (on the corner of King Street, marked with a cross). Passing by, in the middle of the road, a soldier is visible, perhaps making his way to the Khaki Club at No. 11, which stood a few doors before Crosslands, the undertakers.

FROM SMELLING SALTS TO MEDICINAL SNUFF, the High Street branch of W.B. Smith and Son was the place to visit if the Urban Council's continued advocacy of medieval sanitary arrangements got up your nose.

THE PAWNBROKER'S SIGN is suspended over Sidney Smith's premises at No. 7A North Cross Street, while Hart & Co. (Est. 1889), the outfitters, would provide a new suit to hock in hard times. At No. 9, Mrs Cootes boasted of having a 'fancy repository and toy fair', while George Oliver the bootmaker (near right) had evidently diversified. Corbin's, at the other end of the

street, was a competitor. The delivery boy (left) may well have been connected with Bastins the butchers, who traded from two separate shops on this side of the road. Visible in the near and far distance are Hoare and Pilcher (Est. 1902), the house furnishers, and the Blacksmith's Arms on the corner of South Street and Robert's Lane.

ON MISS KELLY'S DOORSTEP (about 1925): Miss Frances Kelly's grocery and sweetshop stood in the High Street next door to Rowe & Co., the high-class tailor, where Woolworth's now stands. Miss Kelly is on the right, with her assistant Miss Russell. (See opposite.)

CROFT'S TOOK OVER Gorman's famous store in Stoke Road in the 1930s, the premises on the left operating as a grocery and confectionery shop while the butchers on the right was accessible by a separate entrance.

KELLY'S HIGH STREET WINDOW (about 1925). Throughout her employment at Kelly's during the 1920s, Miss Russell was not only expected to serve on the counter until 8 or 9 p.m., but was also responsible for deliveries around town and the maintenance of an attractive window display to tempt passers-by. Wages were meagre, averaging five shillings a week (25p), and in a bad week unsold goods were given in lieu. (The windows reflected above the Nuttall's Mintoes belonged to the Old Northumberland opposite.)

MURPHY'S STORES in North Street (opposite The Fox public house) was opened by Henry and Emily Murphy in 1932 and rapidly gained a reputation for stocking anything of any use around the home, including the kitchen sink. Mr Murphy is seen here with some of his wares in the late 1930s.

ROLLS OF LINOLEUM, advertised as 'indestructible', seen here with Mrs Murphy in the 1950s. Murphy's closed in the 1970s, prior to demolition of the North Street area.

All Good Children . . .

THE DETACHED TOWER OF HOLY TRINITY, now dwarfed by blocks of high-rise flats, was Gosport's most prominent landmark for many years. The original church was built in 1696 using money raised from residents, and pews were allocated in accordance with the size of an individual subscription. This raises the interesting question of whether the parishioners at the back could hear that it was they who should inherit the earth.

Alverstoke Church

MANY FAMILIAR SURNAMES are listed on the register of rectors of St Mary's, Alverstoke, reflecting the high status the position carried. Incumbents included Samuel Wilberforce (son of the campaigner against slavery), Charles North (a relation of Prime Minister Lord North) and Thomas Walpole (great-nephew of Sir Robert Walpole).

IN THEIR 'SUNDAY BEST', children of St Mary's Sunday School enjoy a church outing to Stokes Bay in 1908.

THE OLD CHURCH OF ST JOHN THE EVANGELIST at Forton (seen here disused, about 1930) was completed in 1831, though it was soon realized that the population of what was then a hamlet did not justify such an ambitious construction. In 1870 an invitation was extended to the Royal Marines at Forton Barracks to use the church on a regular basis and by 1890 a larger building was being planned to accommodate the swollen congregation.

THE DESCRIPTION of the architecture of the new St John's – 'a building of red Fareham brick with Bath stone dressings in the Early English Style' – sounded better than the completed church looked. It apparently took fourteen years to build.

CHILDREN ARE MARSHALLED outside the Baptist chapel in Grove Road, Hardway, which was built in 1860; this photograph dates from about 1920.

HENRY COOK (1824–93), Wesleyan founder of the Gosport Ragged Day and Sunday School and the Portsmouth and Gosport Seamen's Mission.

THE GOSPORT RAGGED DAY & SUNDAY SCHOOLS ESTᵈ BY H. COOK MAY. 53

FORMER SEAFARER HENRY COOK established a prosperous house-decorating business in the High Street, the stores of which backed on to the poverty-stricken and notorious South Street area. Destitute boys were recruited into Cook's first Sunday school held in these premises, but demand from the slums was such that a free day school was built in South Street from charitable funds in 1853.

THE BETHEL MISSION 'for seamen and the poor' was built in 1869 and incorporated a free day school for girls, intended to keep youngsters off the streets at a time when prostitution was rife. The Mission survived in South Street until its centenary year when it was replaced during extensive redevelopment of the area.

THE INTERIOR OF BETHEL MISSION, about 1925. Note the old coke burner.

STOKE ROAD WESLEYAN (METHODIST) CHURCH was built in 1910–11 to serve the population of the rapidly expanding Newtown. The tower survived a serious fire in 1989.

CHRIST CHURCH was completed in 1865 and the foundation stone of the adjoining Christ Church Institute was laid in 1908, with proceeds from the famous Grove Pageants helping to build and maintain it. The nearby flats in Avenue Road mark the original site of the Baptist Tabernacle which later became The Picturedrome cinema, known irreverently as the 'Tin Tabernacle'.

St. Mark's Church,
Stokes Bay
19376

CONTROVERSY SURROUNDED the construction of St Mark's church, Anglesey, in 1844. Sponsored by Robert Cruickshank and described euphemistically as 'a chapel of ease' to St Mary's, this church appears to have been built to allow the gentry of Anglesey to worship separately from other classes. The structure was found to be unsafe in 1913 and was subsequently demolished.

ROWNER CHURCH, Gosport's oldest, dates from the late twelfth or early thirteenth century, though little remains today of early external features. Restoration work carried out in the 1870s augmented by modernization work in the 1950s was destroyed by fire during improvement work in 1990. (Photograph about 1920.)

FEAR OF GOD was instilled with uncompromising vigour by preacher Sydney Wing, whose dominant presence graced the pulpit of Victoria Street Baptist church for many years (1913).

THE SCENE IN VICTORIA STREET as parishioners attend a re-opening ceremony of the Baptist church following modernization in 1929.

BAPTIST CHURCH SUNDAY SCHOOL children and teachers in the summer of 1906.

SUNDAY SCHOOL TREAT – children set off on their annual outing from Forton Road (about 1910).

ST THOMAS' CHURCH was erected with the aid of a government grant in 1845 to serve the scattered rural communities of Elson and Hardway, with a population (in 1851) of 1,059. Elson Church School was established in 1849.

ST THOMAS' CHURCH HALL, Elson Road (undated). It appears that at some point in its history the features of this interesting building were rationalized in line with ecclesiastical tradition. With the gables made angular and the stacks removed, it now looks like any old church hall.

STALWARTS OF THE TEMPERANCE MOVEMENT, about 1910. Children were transfixed by colourful magic lantern shows about the evils of drink and then dutifully signed a pledge of lifelong abstinence.

THE TEMPTATION offered by Blake's Fine Ales vies with the call of God from the Wesleyan chapel (right) in Priory Road in the 1930s.

THE IMPRESSIVE FAÇADE of St Mary's Roman Catholic church in the High Street was erected at the turn of the century, its architecture cleverly suggesting a powerful grandeur that closer inspection reveals to be illusory.

And so to School

NEWTOWN SCHOOL, classroom interior, about 1927. Built in 1901 to a traditional design, notable features here include the functional but unattractive glossed brickwork (reminiscent of those Victorian underground public conveniences) and high-placed windows (intended to prevent distractions). Paying attention are Gwen Jones, Rosemary Webber, Gwen Shenton, Dorothy Isaac, Gwen Smith, Barbara Prickett.

QUEEN VICTORIA caused considerable disruptions to the schooling of pupils at St Matthew's Schools, the royal train passing close by *en route* for her beloved Osborne. Every time she passed by children were placed alongside the track to sing patriotic songs. The original St Matthew's School was built in 1845 but was extended in 1907. St Matthew's Square itself served as the children's playground.

LEESLAND SCHOOL was opened in 1894 with places for 750 pupils, whose introduction to history began and ended with memorizing salient dates in the acquisition of the British Empire. This photograph is dated 1908 and was taken from outside the Gypsy Queen public house, which was built in 1897.

LEESLAND INFANTS (about 1910). Some teachers evidently permitted a favourite toy to be displayed during class photographs, producing a more interesting and less formal portrait. Clutching a teddy bear, second row down, second from left, is Doris Amelia Tollervey (née Bailey).

SITTING ON THEIR HANDS, infants of Seafield School; fourth from the right is Lilly Challen. Known as 'The Tin School', Seafield was rebuilt and renamed Stone Lane in 1913, but is now Haselworth County Primary.

HOLY TRINITY SCHOOL, shortly after a night air raid in 1944. Pupils were transferred to Clarence Square School, reportedly 'quite unperturbed by the fact that their old school no longer existed'.

GOSPORT & ALVERSTOKE SECONDARY SCHOOL (about 1918). The number of pupils eligible to continue their education at this school was managed by the simple expedient of increasing the fees.

SECONDARY SCHOOL HALL (about 1920). The teacher is believed to be Miss Bell, who taught Physical Exercise. Front row fifth from the right, is Constance Silvester.

BOYS WILL BE BOYS – while fashions change along with theories of education, children remain an irrepressible constant. One boy at St Matthew's Infants (top left) appears to be exploring his nostril with a finger in this photograph dating from about 1900. Note the chalk slate.

THE BOYS AT LEESLAND SCHOOL (about 1925) look innocent enough, despite the stone-sized hole in the classroom window on the right. The headmaster, Mr Taylor (left) and teacher Mr Rundell (right) convey a resigned sense of *déjà vu*. Fourth row, third from the right is Joe Williams.

Leisure and Pleasure

WALPOLE PARK (seen here about 1925) was named after Canon Thomas Walpole, rector of St Mary's, Alverstoke (1846–1881), whose great uncle was Sir Robert Walpole and whose mother was daughter of the second Earl of Egmont and sister of Spencer Perceval, the assassinated Prime Minister. He also had a brother who was Home Secretary and a wife who was a granddaughter of the 5th Duke of Beaufort (see *Gosport Records*, No.10). This twenty-two-acre expanse of land was previously called The Horsefield.

A VIEW FROM THE EAST, about 1920, with Willis Road just visible in the background. Granite setts used in the laying out of Walpole and Gosport Parks were originally used as a road surface from The Hard to Brockhurst Road but were pulled up when electric tramlines were laid in 1903–4. During the two World Wars part of Walpole Park was cultivated as allotments.

THE HISS AND RUMBLE of a traction engine heralded the arrival of Bartlett's Fair (seen here at Stokes Bay, about 1929), a joy to young ears in the days when 'a tanner' would fill a day with cheap thrills and tacky pleasures. Early in May, warning would be given to Camper & Nicholson to remove their logs from The Green in North Street. If help was not forthcoming, Bartlett's mighty engine would be used to drag the obstacles into the sea.

SHOOT A BOTTLE stall at the fair on The Green, in the 1930s. Reportedly the sights on the air rifles (left) were out of alignment. The fair extended from The Green around The Hard to the India Arms Hotel in earlier days.

PRIVETT PARK, about 1955. Poised between makeshift goalposts, Alan Walsh negotiates Brian Dash's shot within window-breaking distance of Privett School. Built in 1937, falling rolls brought demolition in 1982. Parkland Court Estate now occupies the site.

Gosport. Model Yacht Pond.

THE MODEL YACHT POND, seen here in about 1925, was one of several capital works projects set up to provide employment for the heroes of the First World War who had returned to find themselves surplus to requirements. Formerly known as the 'Cocklepond', extensive improvements were made before its formal opening in 1922. Young boys who ached to become apprentices at Camper & Nicholson carved model yachts and tested their theories here.

A ROYAL MARINES' SOCCER MATCH at Forton, dated February 1909. Heading the ball on a wet day was unwise as the uncoated, absorbent leather seemingly doubled in weight.

'ERE COMES THE BOYS BRIGADE, all smuverred in marmalade, A tuppenny a penny pill-box, An' 'alf a yard of braid. . .' (children's song from the 1900s). The aim of this movement, like the Scouts, was to instil discipline and patriotism in working-class boys. This group is seen in South Street in the 1920s.

GOSPORT PARK, seen here in about 1918. For many years Ewer Common, a twenty-seven-acre expanse of furze land, served as an encampment for gypsies, but in 1891 the pressing needs of Gosport & District Cricket Association led to the site being acquired for recreational purposes. Thus, Gosport Park's carefully clipped cricket square, regimented roses and ordered borders displaced unruly nature.

A REDUNDANT CANNON graces Gosport Park on this postcard sent by a Royal Marine camped on Browndown and 'passed by the Censor' in September 1917.

SET ON THE EDGE OF WOODLANDS known as the Wild Grounds, Middle Barn Cottage (seen here in 1947) was for many years the home of Cyril Buckingham who took over as gamekeeper of the Prideaux-Brune Estate in 1927. His main duty was to rear and nurture hundreds of pheasants for the game shoots that his employer took part in annually. Most of the original estate, which stretched from Fort Brockhurst to Stubbington Lane, had disappeared by 1962 to make way for the Rowner Housing Estate. Mr Buckingham died in 1988.

HUNTER MARE 'Kitty' with H.J. Travers in the Crossways, about 1923. The houses (left) front on to Forton Road while the slightly undulating ground to the right spreads, uninterrupted, to the meadows and arable land of Brockhurst, Elson and Hardway.

THE MOAT AT STOKES BAY, about 1906 (note Crescent Road in the background). Built to deter the French in the 1850s, its waters proved a popular attraction for generations of youngsters hopeful of catching crabs and tiddlers. The River Alver flowed into the moat, which was the habitat of nesting swans until the Borough Council filled it in in the 1960s.

A CUP OF TEA AND A CHAT at the women's group meeting, Bethel Mission, South Street, about 1925. Top left is Mrs Maud Russell.

THE CASTLE TAVERN near Gosport Hard. A popular haunt of Gosport's watermen, this public house dates from about 1790 when it was built by brewer Thomas Whitcomb on a site immediately adjacent to Charles Fort (on Gosport Beach). In this photograph from about 1910 the landlord, Mr Gibbs, is seen in the doorway while the inquisitive children of a tenant peer out of the bay window: left to right, Eva, Stanley and Frank Leach.

SMARTLY DRESSED to a man, employees of William Row & Co., the high-class tailor, look forward to a day away from the scissors, chalk, tape measure and ingratiation. Rowe's premises stood a few doors away from the Isle of Wight Hoy public house, seen here in the background. The vehicle is a Provincial charabanc, No. 3, about 1926.

A BARE-KNUCKLED PUGILIST by the name of Arthur strikes a pose for local portrait photographer W.C. Harvey, about 1905. The backcloth that is featured in much of Harvey's work seems intended to suggest a classical, pastoral location, rather than the back room of No. 31 High Street.

IN THOSE CAREFREE DAYS when townsfolk expressed their desire to be at one with nature by picking wild flowers, Grange and Rowner offered something approaching the rural idyll. The curiously named Apple Dumpling Bridge – seen here behind Vicky Curtis in the mid-1930s – points the way to what is now a municipal tip.

'THE FIRST AEROPLANE to make a flight to this district', enthused the *Portsmouth Times* in May 1911, 'flew over Portsmouth from Brighton and descended gracefully and without mishap on the recreation ground at Haslar'. Recognizing the potential of his flying machine, the magnificent pilot, a Mr Gilmour, 'shelled' his brother-in-law, who was stationed at Fort Blockhouse, with oranges. Afterwards, his Bristol biplane proved a popular attraction, drawing sightseers from miles around.

THE GOSPORT BEACH was the starting-point for a ballad, dating from about 1840, concerning the relationship between a sailor and a local prostitute: 'On Gosport Beach I landed, A place of noted fame, I call'd for a bottle of brandy, To treat my bold flash dame, Her outside rigging was all silk, Her spencer scarlet red, We spent the day in pleasure, Til at night we went to bed...' (for remaining verses see *Gosport Records* No. 4, May 1972).

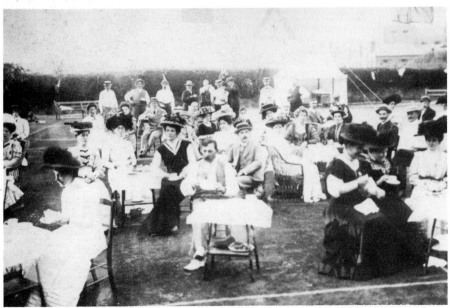

TIME FOR TEA during Gosport and Alverstoke Bowling Club's Ladies' Day, about 1908.

MESSING ABOUT IN BOATS. A poignant wartime photograph taken at Hardway on the eve of the D-Day embarkation in 1944.

THE OLYMPIA ROLLER SKATING RINK was built on the corner of a meadow known as Hobbs' Field at the junction of Queen's Road and Stoke Road. When business declined it was converted into a picture palace but closed in 1935. This photograph dates from about 1915.

The New Foster Gardens Showing Lily Pond Alverstoke. 10.

FOSTER GARDENS about 1955. Note the thatched shelter on the left.

BLACKBERRYING IN ROWNER COPSE, 1908. At the turn of the century Rowner had an indigenous population of 134 and comprised farms and woodland, dotted with the odd cluster of thatched cottages. This rural scene went undisturbed except by the echoing crack of the pheasant shoot, the tell-tale rustle of a snared animal and the rousing call of the Fareham and Gosport Beagles Hunt. Meanwhile, juice-stained little fingers aimed for the mouth rather than the basket.

Open Air Swimming Bath, Gosport 14

THE CENTRAL SWIMMING BATHS, opened in 1924, provided a means of keeping clean for the many inhabitants whose dwellings still lacked an adequate water supply. Limited facilities had previously been available at Thorngate's Charity Washhouse in South Street. Note Flux's Steam Laundry chimney in the background (see p. 103).

STOKES BAY 'COCKLE POND' about 1932. Ella and Dot Mullins lend a helping hand to a reluctant swimmer.

SECTION SEVEN

Out the Bay

A PICNIC ON THE BEACH at Stokes Bay in 1930. The Mullins family is sitting west of the pier; note the swingboats ride next to the 'Boats for Hire' hut.

'ROW, ROW, ROW THE BOAT.' Youthful reflections that 'life is but a dream' were rudely shattered by the calling of your number (Stokes Bay Pier, 1930s).

STOKES BAY PIER, about 1910. Built in 1842, Stokes Bay pier was linked to the Gosport Railway system in 1863, and by 1875 a 2¾-hour service from Waterloo to Ryde via Gosport was advertised. Before long a more direct route was available via Portsmouth Harbour station, and the line closed in 1915.

A RARE AERIAL VIEW, taken in the 1930s. Purchased by the Admiralty in 1922, two cranes (visible here) were installed, reportedly for lifting torpedoes.

THE PROMENADE was constructed in the early 1920s using central government grants and drawing on the pool of willing but unemployed local workers. The pavilion and public conveniences seen here were demolished in 1989.

STOKES BAY DURING THE SCHNEIDER TROPHY RACE for seaplanes in 1929. This photograph was taken by Mr R.A. Lowe, a joiner who helped construct a stand for the thousands of spectators attracted by the sunny weather and the prospect of a British victory.

SOLD OUT. An Eldorado ice-cream vendor, whose pedal-driven ice-box urges potential customers to 'Stop me', awaits the return of his two colleagues with fresh supplies. A scoreboard for the results of the Schneider Trophy Race is visible to the right of the windsock. The race was won by Flying Officer H. Waghorn in a Supermarine powered by a Rolls Royce engine, narrowly beating his Italian rival with an average speed of 328 m.p.h.

THE PIER IS LOST IN A SUNNY HAZE while paddlers soothe their toes in the cool briny. In the days when bicycles could be left unlocked they were evidently hidden behind the beach huts (1910).

EDWARDIAN FAMILY PICNIC, about 1903. Major R.W. Andrew, Border Regiment (Rtd), Commandant and Chief Warden of Forton Military Prison, is sitting on the right (see p. 146).

Down our Road

VIEW OF ELSON ROAD, taken from the corner of Ham Lane, looking west towards St Thomas' church, about 1915.

St. Thomas Road, Gosport.

ST THOMAS'S ROAD. (See opposite.)

ST THOMAS'S ROAD, in about 1935 (above and left). These postcards belong to a set commissioned by Ivy Woodthorpe, proprietor of the newsagent's shop seen on the right. The house on the far right functioned as the police station for Hardway and Elson was the residence of Police Constable Wren for many years (see p. 92). Mutton's grocery store and sweetshop was situated mid-way along the terrace at No. 72.

BURY ROAD, about 1905. High walls and mature trees conceal the residences of the local gentry and professional class . . .

. . . while rows of uniform terraces were erected by speculative builders to house the artisan class in Blake Road, about 1910.

THE RIOT OF ARCHITECTURAL STYLES that was Avenue House, The Avenue, 1926.

ELEMENTAL THATCHED COTTAGE at Rowner Bridge, about 1900.

THE VIEW FROM THE AVENUE looking north towards Bury Cross, about 1908. Bury Grange Farm straddled The Avenue, with grazing land extending back to Bury Hall Lane. (See p. 104.)

PARASOLS IN THE AVENUE, about 1910. This thoroughfare was the only reliable means for vehicular traffic to reach Haslar Hospital and Angleseyville until the opening of Haslar Toll Bridge in 1835 (see p. 94).

PRIVETT ROAD looking east towards Bury Cross, about 1905. From 1906 to 1929 this point marked the end of the electric tram 'Avenue' line (see p. 88).

ANN'S HILL ROAD looking south towards Bury Cross, about 1915; note the Harvest Home public house on the right.

THE REGENCY-STYLE CRESCENT (seen here in 1922) was built in 1830 by Robert Cruickshank as part of his plan to become very wealthy. His scheme involved buying up local farmland cheaply, erecting 'residences fit for the first families in the land' and then promoting the area as a fashionable resort with weather comparable with that of the South of France. His plan fell at the last hurdle.

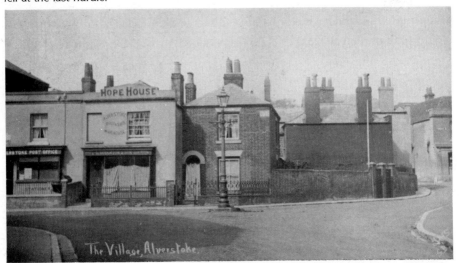

VILLAGE ROAD, ALVERSTOKE, about 1906. Sandwiched between Violet Cottage and the village post office, Hope House was the premises of Houghton's Boot and Shoe Shop.

CRUICKSHANK sought to ingratiate himself with many influential people in his attempt to capitalize on his investments; Angleseyville was named after the Marquis of Anglesey, a one-legged hero of Waterloo who had agreed to take holiday apartments there. The Anglesey Arms Hotel (above) was built by Cruickshank against all advice, and opened on 18 May 1830. His extravagant publicity elicited this response from Lord Hillsborough: 'Thank you for your recommendation of the Hotel. I am glad to hear such a flourishing account of Anglesey. Let Hastings, Brighton, St Leonards and other watering places – Beware.'

CHURCH ROAD, ALVERSTOKE, about 1905. The Five Bells public house (right) served its last pint in 1922.

PRIORY ROAD, about 1935. The housing on the left is of the type erected as part of the policy of rapid expansion of Elson and Hardway in the 1930s, which brought many dockyard workers over from Portsmouth, attracted by cheaper rents.

STOKE ROAD, about 1905. At this time many private residences fronted Stoke Road which was remarkable for its stretch of fine elm trees, lost when the road was widened.

PRIORY ROAD, about 1908. Note the Rose and Crown public house on the left, now the Jolly Roger.

BEACH STREET IN WINTER was overshadowed by yachts laid up for the duration (about 1920).

CHAPEL ROW, looking north, about 1965. Portsmouth power station chimney provides a bearing.

FORTON ROAD, looking west towards St John's, about 1910.

RESIDENCES IN CHAPEL ROW, viewed from Holy Trinity churchyard in 1958.

SPRING GARDEN LANE, about 1908. The first bomb to be dropped on Gosport in the Second World War reportedly fell here in August 1940.

BROCKHURST ROAD, looking north. The Skinner brothers ran a grocery business on the corner of Avery Lane in the 1910s.

BROCKHURST ROAD (undated).

SECTION NINE

Getting About

THE GOSPORT & FAREHAM TRAMWAYS was the trading name for the local operations of the Portsmouth Street Tramways Co. which constructed two routes for their new electric trams: Gosport Hard via Clarence Road, Forton Road, Brockhurst Road, Fareham Road, to Fareham Railway Station; and Gosport Hard via Walpole Road, Stoke Road, over Bury Railway Arch, Foster Road, Bury Road, to Bury Cross (Wiltshire Lamb) (see p. 79).

THE CONSTRUCTION OF THE ELECTRIC TRAMWAYS began in 1903–4 with tracks laid at a standard 4 ft 7 ¾ in gauge. Work is under way here at Gosport Hard, outside the Ferry Tavern (right) and the Castle Tavern (left).

AS STOKE ROAD APPROACHED THE OLD WHITE HART, it forked to either side. To the right (above) the main road climbed sharply over the railway arch with a row of houses below it on the left and an orchard on the right. Bury Arch was demolished in around 1938.

THE LEFT FORK, White Hart Road, led to Gosport Road railway station, viewed here from Cleveland Road. The footbridge or 'Jacob's Ladder' was erected in 1889.

TRAM TERMINUS AT GOSPORT HARD, showing what has been suggested was one of the first journeys of the electric trams in 1906. The days of the horse-bus (seen on the right) were numbered.

THE LAST TRAM TO ANN'S HILL on 29 December 1929. Gosport & Fareham Tramways' operations ceased completely two days later, commemorated by a display of black flags and wreaths on the last ride.

GOSPORT RAILWAY STATION, seen here with its Tuscan colonnade and fenestrated chimneys in about 1890. Built early in the Victorian era to a design by Sir William Tite, it is now a crumbling monument to New Elizabethan neglect.

GATEMEN AT CAMBRIDGE ROAD RAILWAY CROSSING, with a Mrs Higgins, about 1935. These gates were replaced in 1924 and 1938 in consequence of Mr Gould (left) brewing tea, and then again in 1939 when he answered a call of nature.

MODES OF LOCOMOTION in the High Street in the 1930s.

THE BEGINNING OF A LONG TRADITION – one of Gosport's earliest traffic jams is surveyed by PC Wren of Elson at the junction of Brockhurst Road and Military Road in 1929. The occupants of these motionless vehicles are *en route* to Stokes Bay to watch seaplanes flying at 300 m.p.h. over the Solent in the Schneider Trophy Race (see p. 70–71).

THIS SIX-WHEELED Provincial motor bus could accommodate twenty seated passengers.

ECHOING THROUGH THE YEARS, those distinctively nasal but not unmelodic requests to tender your 'Fares, please', 'Hold on tight, please' and 'Move along down the bus, please'.

PROVINCIAL DOUBLE-DECKER BUSES at the Ferry Gardens terminal in about 1960.

HASLAR TOLL BRIDGE. In this photograph from the 1920s the toll house is just visible on the left. Built by Robert Cruickshank in 1835, the history of the bridge is marked, especially in wartime, by expressions of moral indignation that people should have to pay to visit their sick and dying relatives at Haslar Naval Hospital. The bridge itself became a casualty of war during an air raid in 1940.

SECTION TEN

A Working Life

CAMPER & NICHOLSON'S worldwide reputation for building yachts of beauty, elegance and durability relied on the training and the specialized skills of its workers. This photograph shows a group of shipwrights in about 1930.

MEN PREPARING FOR THE LAUNCH of the *Xrifa*, a 278-ton, 90-ft auxiliary ketch, in June 1912.

A TENSE MOMENT for men who took a pride in their work: a view of the stocks during the launch of the *Sylvana*.

THE LAUNCH of the *Xrifa* in 1912. This vessel represented the state-of-the-art in design and comfort. The interior was fitted in mahogany and polished satinwood inlaid with rosewood. Luxurious extras included a refrigerating plant, electric lighting and an electric generator. The client was a Mr Franklin M. Singer, a wealthy American yachtsman.

RATSEY & LAPTHORN supplied many of the sails for Camper & Nicholson's prestigious yachts, including several for America's Cup challengers. It is claimed that the original sails for HMS *Victory* were made in the old Sail Loft at North Wharf, seen here a few years before it was destroyed in an air raid in January 1941.

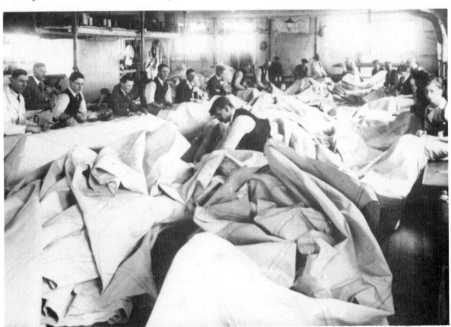

MEN AT WORK on a new sail for the *Astra* (undated).

THE LARGEST SAIL LOFT IN THE WORLD, measuring 150 ft by 45 ft, was contained in this two-storey building erected in 1949.

WOMEN AT WORK cutting a sail on the spreading floor, about 1950.

ROUNDSMEN in Paget Road, Alverstoke, about 1908. Most necessary provisions and domestic articles could be purchased on the doorstep from hawkers or were delivered by local traders, merchants and market gardeners.

BARROW in Clayhall Road, about 1912.

THOMAS BATCHELOR established his coachbuilding and wheelwright's workshop in Clarence Road in the 1880s. Examples of his high standard of workmanship are seen here in about 1900.

ALFRED BATCHELOR continued the tradition in Brockhurst Road, next to Hutfield's Garage on the corner of Harding Road. His business is seen here in about 1916.

FRASER & WHITE, COALMERCHANTS. Workers at Clarence Wharf in the 1890s. Coal was delivered regularly by roundsmen, being an essential fuel for domestic heating and cooking on the kitchen range.

POST OFFICE STAFF in the High Street sorting office during the First World War. Postmaster John Barlow (centre row, fourth from right) lost five of his staff, killed on active service. Women began to be employed in clerical and other jobs previously regarded as male preserves.

FLUX'S GOSPORT STEAM LAUNDRIES LTD in Haslar Street was a major local employer of women for many years. Customers delivered a bag wash to one of Flux's Receiving Offices (in the High Street, Stoke Road and Whitworth Road) and this was returned clean and unironed. Prices were reasonable. Another service on offer was the purification of mattresses.

OVERWORKED AND UNDERPAID, Flux's workers (seen here in 1922) had to contend with a piercing high-pitched whistle throughout their working day, produced by the pressure of gas that was used. Sing-songs helped to relieve the monotony.

BURY GRANGE FARM (about 1908) extended from Privett Road to Bury Hall Lane. Primarily a dairy farm, produce was sold directly through an outlet in the High Street on the corner of Bemister's Lane, and later from another branch in Palmerston Road, Southsea. As with the brewers, there was fierce competition between rival dairies, with frequent accusations of 'watering down' and other malpractices.

MILKMEN DELIVER IN ANGLESEY CRESCENT (about 1908). Milk was transported in churns and the desired amount ladled out at a ha'penny a pint.

THE FORTON DAIRY, about 1909. Hickman's had three local dairies, one at Alverstoke, another in Whitworth Road and these premises at No. 189 Forton Road. Modernized in recent years, it now trades as 'Ye Olde Cobblers Shoppe'.

THE ALVERSTOKE HOUSE OF INDUSTRY where the poor, infirm, blind, crippled, widowed and orphaned were sent to work on a ration of gruel and, among other things, oxheads, under a tyrannical regime that one guardian described, in 1805, as 'erring on the side of humanity'. This photograph was taken during the opening ceremony of the present Alver Bridge, built in 1923 by F. Bevis of Portsmouth using labour drawn from the local unemployed.

THE INTERIOR OF MUMBY'S MINERAL WATER FACTORY, The Green, showing the Bottling and Packing Department in about 1950. Established in the 1850s, water used in the production of Mumby's Soda Water and other products was drawn from an artesian well which penetrated 300 ft beneath their premises.

SHOE AND BOOTMAKER MATTHEW MILLS (right), from Huddersfield, set up his 'Yorkshire Boot Repairers' shop in Clarence Road in 1890, establishing a family business that continues to this day, in Stoke Road. This photograph, dating from the turn of the century, raises the problematic choice of an appropriate collective noun for old cobblers.

WHERRYMEN PLY THEIR TRADE off The Hard in about 1910. Within ten years this traditional local calling had all but disappeared, the grunting heave of oars having been replaced by the easy chug of steam ferries.

MAKING HAY WHILE THE SUN SHINES in Elson, August 1929. The old vicarage wall is just visible to the right, suggesting that Brighton, Worthing and Selsey Avenues were built on the farmland seen here in the middle and foreground.

Community Matters

THE OLD FIRE STATION was erected in 1901–2 on the corner of Clarence Road and North Street, next door to Millard's the Corn Merchant (left). Purpose-built, it comprised an engine room, Superintendent's office, living quarters and duty room. In the absence of other means of raising alarm the look-out tower afforded a panoramic view of the area.

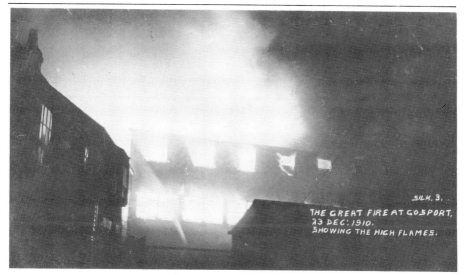

THE GREAT FIRE OF GOSPORT, as it became known, broke out in a warehouse at Camper & Nicholson's yard, eliciting a quick response from the horse-drawn brigade, closely followed by an estimated 10,000 spectators. There were several serious casualties among Superintendent Mortimore's heroic fire-fighters.

FIRE ENGULFED THE SOLDIERS' INSTITUTE in Forton Road, opposite Inverness Road, in 1908. Erected in 1888 of wood and galvanized iron this structure was soon razed to the ground in spite of the efforts of Mortimore's brigade. Concern was expressed at the time about the lack of adequate equipment and resources to tackle blazes which inevitably put lives and property at risk. A replacement Home for Soldiers and Sailors was opened at York House in Clarence Square in 1910.

THE ISOLATION HOSPITAL in Ham Lane, Elson was built in 1889 on a three-acre plot by Gosport brewer Thomas Blake, providing accommodation for thirty-four patients. This block comprised enteric and scarlet fever wards. With the advantage of good food, warm clothing, cleanliness and comfortable living conditions, some children recovered to return to their homes. Additional bed space for twelve smallpox sufferers was added in 1900. Blake's now serves the community as a maternity hospital.

THE ISOLATION HOSPITAL LAUNDRY BLOCK (about 1889).

THE ISOLATION HOSPITAL ADMINISTRATION BLOCK (about 1889). The nursing staff consisted of a matron, a charge nurse, nine unqualified nurses, a cook, two maids, two laundry women, a gardener and a caretaker.

THE WAR MEMORIAL HOSPITAL, photographed from the roof of Bury House in the 1950s. Bury Cross Water Works' 80-ft high red-brick water tower, built in 1866 and demolished in 1970, is on the left. The old Harvest Home and Cheriton Road Estate are on the right.

HASLAR HOSPITAL about 1909. In the late nineteenth century rails were laid from the landing jetty at Blockhouse Lake into the main arcade of Haslar, facilitating an efficiently managed wartime traffic of hand-pushed carts laden with sick and wounded marines and sailors (see p. 61, p. 136).

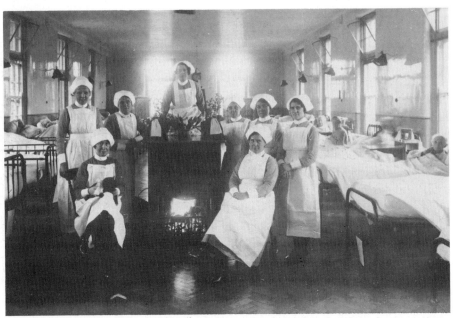

A GROUP OF GOSPORT NURSES (undated).

THE BOYS IN BLUE. Gosport Police, about 1930.

THE OLD TOWN HALL in the days when the rateable value of one's property was seen as the most equitable means of financing community services.

BURY HOUSE (seen here about 1880) was a focal point for seances and experiments in mystical alchemy in Victorian times. Wealthy resident Thomas South and his daughter Mary shared a passionate belief in ancient religions and devoted themselves to the age-old search for a method of transforming base metals into silver and gold. This was possible, they believed, by sheer mind power rather than chemical transmutation. But when Mary published a study of alchemy in which she claimed to have seen this succeed, Mr South bought back every copy he could find, fearing rejection from polite society.

IN BURY HOUSE GROUNDS (above) stacks of Mary's books were transmuted into ash in a giant bonfire, though one copy survived and was later republished. Shortly after the Second World War the near-derelict Bury House was acquired by the newly formed Gosport Community Association.

THE VIEW BEHIND BURY HOUSE before work began on the construction of the new community centre, the Thorngate Halls, in the 1950s.

COMMUNITY ASSOCIATION VOLUNTEERS: this group includes Jack Scard (crouching), 'Pop' Graham, Alderman H.T. Rogers and Fred Smith.

FUND RAISING Carnival float in the 1950s.

ALDERMAN ROGERS (mayor 1955–57) speaking at the foundation-stone laying ceremony.

The Refuge

TOWARDS THE END OF THE LAST CENTURY, Thomas Stephenson, a Wesleyan minister based in Lambeth, became so appalled by the poverty and living conditions in his parish that he resolved to do what he could for at least some of the slum children who were 'ragged, shoeless, filthy, their faces pinched with hunger and premature wretchedness'. In 1887 some land was donated to Stephenson's cause by a Mr Diggle of Alverstoke, and work began on building suitable accommodation for the 'mites of children to whom death apparently could alone show kindness'. But precarious reliance on the whim of charity enabled help and convalescence to be offered to only a small number of those who needed it.

CONVALESCENCE COULD BE FUN when taking the sea air from a pony and trap, though the ethos of the Children's Home, as exemplified by this monocled matron, precluded unseemly exuberance. (Photograph dated 1909.)

LADY WAKEFIELD HOUSE, about 1930. Benefactor Lord Wakefield was associated with the home for many years, acting as its treasurer. Believed to be the first house built by Robert Cruickshank in what was to become Angleseyville, the foundation stone was laid by the Earl of Uxbridge in 1826 and the building was known as Uxbridge House until its acquisition by the Children's Home in 1930.

ATKINSON HOUSE, about 1930. Utilized as an administration block, this was named after Sister Margaret Atkinson who was Superintendent of the home for many years.

THE INTERIOR OF STEPHENSON HOUSE, about 1936. Included in this carefully posed photograph are Nancy Little and Molly Pinner. Proceeds from the sale of this postcard went to the home.

SUNSHINE HOUSE (about 1935) was a purpose-built sanitorium erected in the early 1930s after a nationwide appeal for funds.

THE HOSPITAL (note Gilkicker on left). During the two World Wars the Children's Home was commandeered as a centre for the reception of the sick and wounded. Over 1,000 patients were admitted during the First World War, with additional bed space being provided at the Brodrick Hall and Brookfield House. Many were severe cases of malaria, trench foot and gas poisoning.

PIGGOTT HALL, about 1930.

DAISY HOUSE, about 1930.

THORNEYCROFT & HORNESLEA HOUSES, about 1930. In the late 1970s the home provided refuge for Vietnamese 'boat people', but by 1984, despite a campaign to 'Save Our Home' by child residents, the building and grounds were sold for redevelopment.

Putting out the Flags

THE PROCLAMATION OF KING GEORGE V, announced from the steps of the Thorngate Hall in May 1910. The King's Royal Rifles Band played 'God Save the King'; there were three cheers for King George and one for Queen Mary, but the heartiest came from the children when it was announced that schools would be closed for the day.

ST JOHN AMBULANCE BRIGADE. Members subjected their royal visitor, Princess Henry of Battenburg, to 'a very realistic demonstration of ice accidents and resuscitation from drowning' at the Connaught Drill Hall in August 1907.

DURING THE CORONATION CELEBRATIONS OF 1911, Martin Collins is seen outside his frame-making shop in Forton Road. On display are a range of souvenirs to mark the occasion. Established in 1894, Mr Collins' business was patronized by artist Martin Snape of Spring Garden Lane. Deliveries were effected using the cart seen here, accompanied by Dorothy, Martin and Henry, who then enjoyed a ride home. The business continued in Dorothy's hands until the early 1980s.

THE LAUNCH of Sir Thomas Lipton's *Shamrock IV* from Camper & Nicholson's stocks in May 1914 was an admirably stage-managed affair; it was the Queen's birthday, the flags were out, the warships were dressed in Portsmouth Harbour and the *Victory* fired a royal salute only a few minutes before the *Shamrock* struck the water.

MILLIONAIRE GROCER SIR THOMAS LIPTON was a shrewd businessman and pioneering self-publicist whose challenges for the America's Cup were estimated to yield a fifty per cent return on his investment. Secrecy surrounded the building of *Shamrock IV* lest details of its design reach the American competitors. The publicity value of this secrecy was not lost on Lipton, who announced that no married man at Camper & Nicholson's was to be allowed to work on the construction. 'They would', he insisted, 'gossip to their wives'. The wisdom of this embargo was debated in the national press throughout the 'silly season' of 1914.

UMBRELLAS RATHER THAN FLAGS greeted the French Fleet when it entered Portsmouth Harbour in 1905 to help consolidate the spirit of friendship and trust enshrined in the recently signed *Entente Cordiale*.

GOSPORT CARNIVAL PARTICIPANTS prepare for the parade at St George's Barracks in the late 1940s.

HIGH STREET CARNIVAL in the late 1940s. At the reins is Henry Murphy, proprietor of Murphy's Stores in North Street. Gosport Theatre is on the right.

In Defence of the Realm

THE ROYAL MARINE LIGHT INFANTRY – known as the 'Red Marines' – was moved from Clarence to Forton Barracks in 1848. The story goes that the last unit to leave smuggled an old clock across the water and installed it over the main gate of their new home as a souvenir, hence the Royal Marine tradition, 'The last man out takes the clock'. However, close examination of the clock – made by Gillette & Johnson of Clerkenwell – suggests that it was not made before 1860.

FORTON BARRACKS at the junction of Mill Lane and Forton Road, about 1910. Completed in 1807, the barracks was the most important factor in the expansion of what had previously been the rural hamlet of Forton. Not unconnected with this new presence was the establishment of a refuge 'for fallen and friendless girls' in Forton Road.

FORTON BARRACKS (about 1910) proudly boasted the largest parade ground in the country, keeping quiet about its dire acoustics.

SERGEANTS' MESS DINING ROOM: interior (undated).

'OUR HOUSE' ON BROWNDOWN, about 1909. As well as routine manoeuvres, annual musketry contests were held on the ranges here between rival divisions.

APART FROM PRACTICAL APPLICATIONS, activities such as bridge-building fostered that essential team spirit.

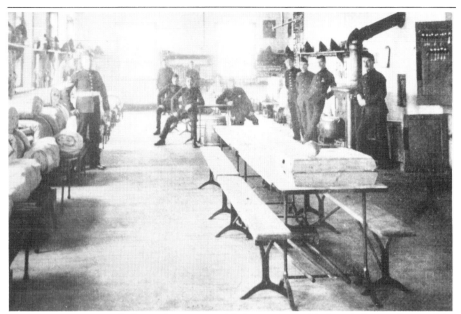

THE SPARTAN INTERIOR of a barrack room provided a contrast with the relative opulence of the Sergeants' Dining Room (p. 133).

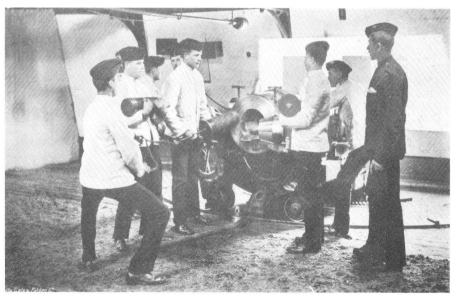

EACH MAN *becomes* part of the gun. Loading a 9.2 BL Gun at Forton Barracks in about 1909.

HEADED BY THE RMLI BAND, some of the survivors of the famous Zeebrugge Raid of April 1918 are given a rousing welcome by residents lining Forton Road. Of the 170 local marines who took part in the raid, 131 returned.

GREAT TO BE ALIVE: survivors of the First World War celebrate peace on earth and goodwill to all men at Haslar, Christmas, 1919.

MILITARY MEMORIAL CARD, dated 1922. Such ceremonials were only practised in peace-time for logistic reasons.

THE BROWNDOWN LANDSCAPE has remained unchanged for centuries, featureless and tranquil but for the occasional rude interruption from the military (for testing weaponry) and duellists hopeful of retaining both their honour and their lives (the last public duel fought in England took place here in 1845). This passing group of military gentlemen was captured with a transient backdrop of warships in 1908.

BLOCKHOUSE FORT, a rare early view taken from Portsmouth in 1864. By 1879 the potential for underwater warfare had begun to be recognized and a sea-mining base was set up here, but by 1905 the Royal Navy's first submarine base was established amid reservations that such war machines were 'damned un-English'.

SUBMARINE SQUADRON at HMS *Dolphin*, about 1930.

138

HMS *ST VINCENT*, school entrance, about 1947. The original HMS *St Vincent* was launched in 1814 and after a distinguished career spent its retirement serving as a boys' training ship in Portsmouth Harbour (1862–1906). Forton Barracks was commissioned as a training establishment in 1927, following the transfer of the RMLI to Eastney in 1923.

SINK OR SWIM. Held afloat by lifelines a young sailor learns to swim, seemingly contradicting stories that boys were mercilessly 'thrown in at the deep end'. Recruits were provided with lodgings at the St Vincent Boys' Home in South Street, under the watchful eye of a Miss Kissock.

ST VINCENT DISPLAY TEAM perform on the New Barracks field in the 1930s.

THE *ST VINCENT* BUGLE BAND in 1947. The band led route marches through Gosport, although the editor of *St Vincent* Magazine complained that 'some of the local horses do not appreciate [their] efforts and it has been necessary to stop playing whilst passing these restless beasts'.

HEROES OF THE STRIKES, about 1911. Serious grievances about pay and conditions in many industries led to a period of demonstrations and strikes in the years leading up to the First World War. Troops, including a detachment from the New Barracks, were used to break the spirit of national labour unrest and resulted in a number of fatalities. Despite the caption attached to this group, pictured on their barrack-room steps, many soldiers had mixed feelings about their role.

THE NEW BARRACKS GUARDROOM about 1900. The New Barracks was taken over by the Royal Navy in 1941 and became known as HMS *Victory IV* and then HMS *St George* Barracks.

ST. VINCENT V WINCHESTER COLLEGE.

A STRONG EMPHASIS ON SPORTS ensured a ship-shape crew. The curriculum included water polo, cross-country running, boxing, hockey, rifle shooting, rugby and soccer. Football matches were arranged with local teams including Alverstoke Lads, Aylings Bakery and St John Ambulance.

ST VINCENT BAND MARCH PAST, High Street, about 1947.

GERMAN PRISONERS OF WAR in Forton Road in August 1914. Soldiers from the New Barracks (later St George) formed a military guard and marched the 120 German sailors from the Royal Clarence Yard to Fort Elson for imprisonment.

A LOCAL JOURNALIST OBSERVED, 'The prisoners were all in civilian attire and looked typical Teutons. They appeared to be very happy and contented with their lot . . .'

FIRST WORLD WAR MUNITION BADGES of the type worn at Priddy's Hard Naval Ordnance Depot (actual size).

GOSPORT MUNITION WORKERS during the First World War. Local women were employed in large numbers at Priddy's Hard, often on hazardous work like shell and cartridge filling, TNT bagging, and work on mines and depth charges. One of the perils associated with shell filling was toxic jaundice caused by TNT poisoning. This condition turned the workers' faces a repulsive yellow, earning them the nickname of 'the canaries'.

TRENCHES OUTSIDE THE TOWN HALL. During the First World War the citizens of Gosport contributed nearly a million pounds to the war effort. This photograph dates from 1918 when mock trenches, artillery and a biplane were displayed outside the Town Hall to publicize 'Gun Week' during which money was raised to provide munitions for 'Tommy' and 'Jolly Jack' to 'finish the job'.

SOLDIERS OF THE ROYAL GARRISON ARTILLERY outside an ivy-covered Sergeants' Mess, Fort Brockhurst in October 1914.

FORTON MILITARY PRISON, built in around 1850, represented the most up-to-date Victorian ideas of penal reform, with troublesome inmates being buried alive in dark, suffocating underground cells. A breath of fresh air was introduced with the arrival of Commandant R.W. Andrews at the turn of the century and prisoners, including Boer War POWs, were trained in useful trades and given regular exercise. This institution, comprising 150 cells and warders' quarters, was closed in 1927 and a working men's club and flats now occupy the site in Leesland Road.

CHRISTMAS DAY AT FORT MONCKTON, 1907. The Royal Engineers were stationed at Fort Monckton from 1892 until 1928. From 1905 the unit specialized in searchlights and was named the School of Electric Lighting. Behind the rather staid group at the table, two less inhibited soldiers, glasses in hand, appear to be enjoying a carouse while a third plays the piano.

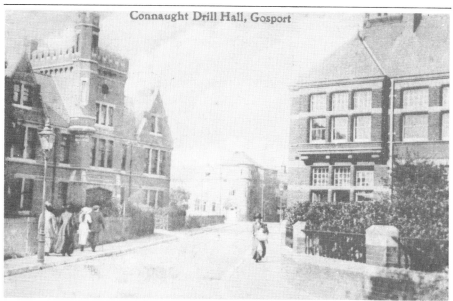

THE CONNAUGHT DRILL HALL (about 1910). Built in 1902, the hall served as a focal point for military and community activities for many years. Gosport Library now occupies the site.

BURNEY'S ACADEMY, Clarence Square (undated). Established in 1791 by Dr William Burney, the Academy aimed to prepare sons of the nobility and gentry for military, naval and diplomatic careers. Although it closed in 1905, Burney's philosophy of education, training and character development reached its natural apogee in the First World War.

WAR WORKERS AT PRIDDY'S HARD, 1944. During the Second World War the number of ordnance workers employed here had trebled to nearly 4,000 including some 1,700 women, who normally worked a twelve-hour day from 7 a.m. to 7 p.m. This group was employed on fitting fuses, a particularly hazardous occupation because of the explosive and toxic nature of the materials used.

The Big Bad Wolf

DURING THE SECOND WORLD WAR there were sixty-one air raids on Gosport. Over 11,000 properties were damaged and nearly 500 completely destroyed. The civilian death toll numbered 111, and 289 were injured. Above, Hartingdon Road. Below, North Close, Alverstoke.

WARTIME FIREMEN with a Dennis fire-engine outside Alverstoke Workhouse in 1940. Inmates were evacuated after a bomb destroyed the boiler house and workhouse chimney. (Included in this group are: Absolum, Stringer, Chase, Carroll, Rouse; Captain Willoughby is on the right.)

FIRE BRIGADE INSPECTION – this photograph was taken from the steps of the Thorngate Hall, gutted in the Blitz of 1941.

GOSPORT & FAREHAM FIREFIGHTERS outside the Forum Cinema in Stoke Road, about 1944. (Front row, third from right, Thomas Challen.)

DAD'S ARMY: Gosport Home Guard march past the Gas Company offices in the High Street, about 1941.

BEACH STREET (see p. 12).

SOUTH STREET, looking towards High Street.

MAYFIELD ROAD. Note the Anderson shelter on the left.

SOUTH STREET.

PORTLAND PLACE, South Street.

MARINA BUILDINGS, corner of Stoke Road and St Edward's Road.

AVENUE ROAD.

PAIN & MARSH, High Street (see pp. 20, 21).

GERMAN PRISONERS OF WAR at work on building Bridgemary Estate, 1945.

BRAVING GOSPORT'S AERIAL DEFENCES, Father Christmas made it to the Connaught Drill Hall to distribute traditional wooden toys to wide-eyed children made homeless by the 'Big Bad Wolf'.

SUNSET OVER GOSPORT, 1949.

PHOTOGRAPHERS AND PHOTOGRAPHIC PUBLISHERS featured in this compilation:

Aymotte • D.W. Baker • H.J. Bond • Blake • G.C. Cozens • Stephen Cribb
Gale and Polden • W.C. Harvey • J.C. Lawrence • Lindley Series • Maynard's
Series • Pamlin Prints • Photochrom Co. Ltd • Portsmouth & Sunderland
Newspapers • Parker Series • Reginald Silk • William Smith • W.W. Spiers
Spithead Series • Eric Stewart • A.H. Sweasey • Topic • Valentine's
J. Welch & Sons • Woolstone Bros.

ACKNOWLEDGEMENTS

Grateful thanks to the following individuals, institutions and businesses for their assistance in the compilation and research of this volume:

Peter Rogers (whose idea it was) • David Kemp and Paul Rogers of Gosport Museum • Kiran Shaughnessy and Alison Clennell of Gosport Library (Hampshire County Council) • The Staff of Portsmouth Central Library (Hampshire County Council) • The Portsmouth *News* • Radio Solent, Ocean Sound, *Streetlife, The Journal* • Pamlin Prints • Mr Mills of F. Mills, Shoe Repairs & Leather Goods, 95 Stoke Road • Mr W.R. Bowles • Mr & Mrs Norman W. Collins • Vera Curtis • Mrs Dines • Mrs Olwin Farley and the late Arthur Farley, fireman. • Mrs D. Goodwin • Mr & Mrs Len and Ella Hadenham Mrs Hague • Mr & Mrs Cecil and Elsie Harbut • Mrs Hawkins • Mrs Herbert Connie Hooker • Gwen Jones • Mrs Leach • Mr R.A. Lowe • Barry McCann Vera Malloy • Mr & Mrs Bernard and Lillian Mullins • Mr G. O'Neill of Gosport Community Association • Mrs J. Plummer • Susan Sargent Wendy Saunders • Mr R. Travers-Bogusz • Mrs Vear • Mrs Dorothy Williams Mr & Mrs Charles Willoughby • Betty Wright

SOURCES

The Portsmouth *Evening News* files
Hampshire Telegraph files
Portsmouth Times files
Kelly's Directories
The *Gosport Records* and other publications of The Gosport Society.
The *Down Memory Lane* series of books and articles by Ron Brown
The Story of Gosport by Dr L.F.W. White
The memories of the people of Gosport.